Joan Taylor

Don Bakely (signature)

If...
a big word with
the poor

Donald C. Bakely

Photographs by Terry Evans

Library of Congress Catalog Card Number 75-35305
International Standard Book Number 0-87303-343-4

Copyright ©1976 by Faith and Life Press
724 Main Street, Newton, Kansas 67114

Photographs copyright ©1976 by Terry Evans, Salina, Kansas
67401

Printed in the United States of America

Design by John Hiebert

This book is dedicated to:

Jesus Christ,
       who
            still teaches us to love
                 those who hit the jackpot in life,
                 those who didn't,
                   and
                 those who never will;

Jeanne,
       my wife and best friend,
           who
               warms my days,
               puts poetry in my life,
                 and
               loves me
                     in
                        spite
                           of everything;
and to—

my parents,
　　who
　　　　were smart enough to raise me poor—but not poorly,
　　who
　　　　set me in my ways solidly enough
　　　　　　to handle a job
　　　　　　　　and a life
　　　　　　　　　　like this one,
　　and who
　　　　were wise enough to teach me to be open
　　　　　　　　　　　　to
　　　　　　　　　　　all
　　　　　　　　　　　　people;

and, of course,
　　to the poor of America and our world
　　who
　　　deserve a better break,
　　and among whom
　　　　we hide
　　　　　　and suppress
　　　　　　much
　　　　　　　of our country's greatness.

Foreword

By United States Senator
James B. Pearson

Conventional wisdom has it that the world is really a cold, cruel place in which to live. But for most Americans that simply is not true.

To be sure, many in the United States face the bleak prospect of more poverty, of slum housing, of a poor diet, and of inadequate medical care. They are the primary victims of rising crime rates. And they suffer most from inflationary spirals and cycles of recession.

But the majority of Americans enjoy, and will continue to enjoy, good jobs and comfortable homes. For these, the cold cruel world exists only in newspaper headlines and television film clips.

The poetry and pictures contained in this book are not about the good life—the life of the two-car garage, the air-conditioned home, and the color television. Instead they chronicle the short and simple annals of the poor.

Terry Evans and Don Bakely have combined their many talents to produce this poignant and sensitive volume. You will find Ms. Evans' message etched as firmly in your mind as on her negatives. And the pathos of the poor, gleaned from a quarter century of ministering to their needs, fills the Reverend Bakely's poetry. These vignettes will no doubt fascinate you as they have fascinated me. They are filled with compassion and understanding.

This book is about the society in which we live. That the message is not always pleasant goes without saying; it reveals in a thousand subtle ways the shortcomings of this land.

It is appropriate that such a volume should first be published during America's Bicentennial, for it is not only a time to celebrate our proud heritage but also a time to renew promises that we have yet to keep.

6

The creators of this work have given us a vivid portrait of another America. It is a poverty portfolio. The pages brim with the quiet and dignified lives of poor people doing ordinary things. These are our neighbors. And through this book we can feel compassion for them and understand their problems in a very personal way—a way that lifeless social statistics can never provide.

Washington, D.C.
October 1975

To set the tone

Almost every book has a reason for existing. This book is being written as an attempt to make a small dent in America's mind about my people, the poor.

The dent needs to be made.

In my job, I have occasion to travel throughout America, speaking in small villages, large and small cities, rural areas and suburbs. As I travel, I listen. As I listen, I have heard many good Americans say many bad words about the poor.

I've noticed that many of these complaints have little to do with facts. One of the favorites, for instance, is this one: "Welfare people? They're all a bunch of lazy men who would rather get a free paycheck than work." Actually the truth is nowhere near that statement. When that statement was most popular, I remember reading the government's figures which showed that of people on welfare, only 0.9 percent were unemployed but employable men. When that figure is turned around, it shows that 99.1 percent of all the people are *not employable* males.

Many harmful generalizations are made by all people. My people do it, too: "Those people in the suburbs got it made. They don't have any problems; they just *make* problems for us."

A lot of us seem to feel that if we can lump people together in general terms and lay evil on them, that excuses us from caring about them. If we can convince ourselves that all poor people are lazy bums, that gets them off *our* backs. The fault, we say, lies with *them,* not us. Hate and distrust seem to be easier for us to handle when we can categorize others.

In this book, I'm trying to uncategorize the poor. I'm trying to put faces on my people. I want you to see them as individuals, as people with joys, pains, hopes, and often overwhelming problems. I want you to see some of the traps they are in, feel some of the things they feel. I want you to walk with them just a little bit and try to see some of their almost impossible situations.

Why poetry?

I see poetry as the language of emotion. I also see poverty as an *emotional,* not a *rational,* issue. If poverty *were* a rational issue, we wouldn't make irrational statements about it, such as referring to all welfare people as "lazy bums."

I'd like to get to your logic

through your emotions. If readers can feel some of the things my people feel, if through this book Terry and I can put faces on the poor for you, then perhaps it will be more difficult for America to dismiss the poor so easily.

In this volume, I'm aiming at two things: understanding and compassion. I feel that *understanding* is a severely limited capacity for most of us. Let me explain. For twenty-five years I've been married to the best person I know. We've argued and dealt with each other for a long time; we've molded each other. Yet, after twenty-five years, I don't *understand* her. I don't know if I ever will—or can. The ability to understand doesn't remove the tensions between us. I can never walk in her shoes, feel her pain or frustrations, hear her thoughts. What makes our life a good one isn't a limited *understanding*; it's love that makes a difference, that fills in the gaps.

I want you to understand as much as you can about the poor. But I want you to go past that. As you see their faces, as they become individuals, I want you to learn to care.

The pictures tell their own stories. Some of them fit with the poems, and some of them inspired poems. As I write, I'm not trying to put words in the mouths of the individuals in the pictures. Some of the people pictured are personal friends; some I don't even know. I can't speak for them. What I can do is gather together words and feelings from years of association with the poor and attempt to get some of those feelings on paper. I hope that the pictures give a more intense emphasis to what is written, and that the words give a more intense emphasis to the pictures.

As you look through the book, notice how many of the pictures look as though they were taken decades ago. Actually, every one was taken within the past few years. One of the marks of poverty is that the poor are always several decades behind the affluent. They live in houses with equipment from some other decade. Their clothes and cars are often from some past decade. Even their medicine (home remedies) and education seem unsuited to today. Their skills and jobs are often those used before we got into such a technical society. You can almost tell the depth of their poverty by putting their skills and possessions in the year in which they belong.

The *very* poor still chop wood to heat their homes, walk because they have no cars, use herbs instead of medicine, have a third-grade education, live in primitive hovels. The *less* poor have untrustworthy cars, gas space heaters, deteriorating homes, a grammar-school educa- tion. The *low-income* families live in projects or in homes two or three times removed from the affluent. They got into high school, their stoves and equip- ment are always on the verge of breaking down, cars are seven years old.

The *affluent,* however, have the things of today (except for the nostalgia and antique fads): new cars, equipment, education, jobs using today's techniques, living in the newer settlements. They talk about today's issues, using recent information.

Poverty, then, is almost a chronological thing. The poor seldom fit; they seldom are wel- come in our world of today. We even call whole peoples "back- ward nations."

As you learn to know the poor, it's possible that you can see how easily many of them could be brought into this decade.

Other things are in these poems. As a United Methodist minister, I have spent almost all of the twenty-five years of my ministry in the inner city, among poverty people. I pastored a church which worked many

years in the slums of Camden, New Jersey, among the poor. It served hundreds of kids that organized into fight gangs in order to have "families" that could be depended on. It worked with skid row, prostitutes, people in trouble, people in pain. For the last ten years I have been director of Cross- Lines Cooperative Council in Kansas City. This is a volunteer agency through which we have been able to pull together the resources of hundreds of church- es, agencies, business people; affluent and poor—blacks, whites, and Mexican Americans—in an effort to eliminate poverty and break down barriers that exist between people. I speak some two hundred to three hundred times a year to national, region- al, and local groups all over this country in an effort to get people to see the poor as they really are, to give themselves and their resources in ways that will open doors for the poor. I've worked among poverty people just about all of my adult life.

But, I grew up in it, too. I watched my father—a strong, hardworking, caring man—as he gave all his powers to keep us fed in the bad days. He is in many of these poems. I remem- ber my mother's attempts to help us not feel so poor. When we had no food, she showed us a newspaper picture of starving kids in India—I still remember their faces—and explained to us that hunger was what *they* were experiencing; we'd probably eat before too long, but they wouldn't. I remember her constantly giving to others even when we didn't have enough for ourselves. I remember her complete hope that tomorrow would be better.

I watched my sister, Joyce, raising four small children in a shack in Georgia. Her husband died leaving her destitute at the age of twenty-nine, yet with a deep faith in Jesus Christ that brought her through it all. I watched another sister, Anita, who with her husband had broken away from poverty, until an accident almost destroyed his leg. It took so long to heal that he lost his compensation, job, and home. It took years and a very determined spirit for them to recapture what they had lost because of one accident.

Someone else who enters these poems is a very special gift that God gave our family. Our fifth child (out of six) was born severely retarded. Never in his life could he walk or talk or sit up or hold anything in his hand or even hold his own head up.

He changed our family.

Inside that nonworking body was one of the great inventions of God. He forced us to concentrate on giving to him rather than just filling our own needs. Kids from the fight gangs loved him, because for many of them his was the first body they had ever been able to press against theirs without getting smacked, cussed, or shoved away. He needed constant care, and they benefited by giving it to him. There were those in our society who suggested, in veiled ways, that it was a shame that such a child lived to drain others, to cost others, to use others.

No one is useless.

Certainly not my son. What he gave us by *being* was not measurable.

Certainly not the poor. I take it personally when suggestions are made that the poor should not be allowed to exist, or should be aborted, or be dispensed with.

I was born and raised poor— and I feel that my life is valid, that in some small way, it is important for me to be here.

Do I care for the poor more than for the affluent?

No.

Then why do I emphasize the poor? Because I know them better. Because the affluent already have plenty of good public relations going for them. We

already look up to them as the
brightest and the best, as "the
way people ought to be."

One thing, however, that is not
lifted up enough about the afflu-
ent is their sense of goodness.
America tends to see them as
responsible (they have jobs and
don't drain us with welfare) but
somewhat selfish. If it weren't
for the commitment, sharing,
concern, and spirituality of many
of the affluent, we couldn't
do what we do at Cross-Lines.

No one is worthless. People
are not to be eliminated from
our love just because we want to
fit them into categories. God's
love is for all of us. So must it
be with our love.

Don Bakely

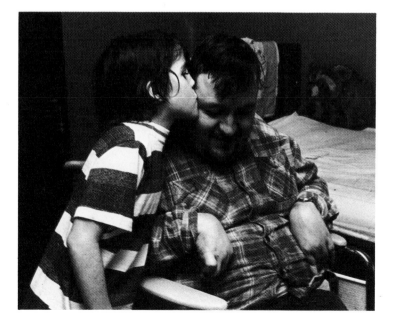

Thanks

Very few books are written in a vacuum—by the one person who gets his name listed as the author. Lots of people shoved me into this book and made it happen.

For instance, there is the Cross-Lines Board of Directors (my bosses) who seemed happy to get rid of me for most of a year while I went off to hide and write.

There is Myron Dice, program director of Cross-Lines, who picked up most of my responsibilities that year and piled them on top of his eighty-hour week (and he doesn't even *like* my job). There is Joy Clark, secretary, surrogate mother of the staff, and runner of the office, who was kind enough to act as if she missed me while I was on Cape Cod, "goofing off" and writing.

There are Professor Chuck Moore and his wife, Jackie, and their family who took a sabbatical from his job at the college in Worthington, Minnesota. He knew I'd have some conscience qualms about dumping my load on the rest of the staff for a year. His decision to come helped me make my decision to go.

The rest of my staff is made up of excellent people—most of

whom are full-time volunteers from all over the country. They encouraged me to stay away longer, and worked hard at keeping my ego pumped up. When I returned from my sabbatical, there was a big, respectful sign on my office door that said, "We're glad you're back, Big Daddy!" It was signed by each of the staff members with such loving thoughts as, "It couldn't get any worse anyway. Alan"; "But not very often. Karen"; "Some of us anyway. Barbara"; "Undecided. Lorene"; "There are days, though. Joy"; and "Good, I'll sic all those people on *you*. Myron." As you can imagine, I run a tight ship and command a great deal of awe among my fellow workers.

Actually, there *are* people who had a real impact on the writing of this book—people like Pop Knoche, eighty-six-year-old director of Loyalty Mission, who stayed poor all his life to help the poor, and who with his life gives a new meaning to the word "great"; Helen Harper who in her thirties rose from poverty to become the director of the "poverty program" and volunteer president of Cross-Lines; Paul Davis and Fay Williams whose constant concern for their pov-

14

erty neighbors continually turns into a gusher of energy and action.

Reaching into the past, there were Dr. Harry Hummer, a seminary professor, and the Reverend "Chic" Hawk and his wife, Betty, who set tones in my life which have continued to affect me.

And especially, there is Terry Evans whose camera mirrors her deep sensitivity and whose pictures say so many things for which I couldn't find words.

D.C.B.

If... a big word with the poor

Lord,

I don't know if
    You
        are up to listening
           to
        the likes of me.

That's why
    I haven't been
        bothering You much.

See,
    sometimes I figure
        that
    -if I'm not good enough for my caseworker to give me the time of day,
    -and if a cop only sees me as a potential problem,
    -and a doctor sees me as somebody to get over with in a hurry,
    -and even the damn trashman doesn't want to stop by my house,
then
    I must be far too sorry a person
        to be a bother
         to You.

But, I'm caught, see?
    I know that the difference between them
                and You
    is that *they* don't give a damn—
        and
           it's different with You!

Even though You've got
    the universe
        on Your hands,
    I understand
        You care.

And

    with *all* the things bothering You in the universe
        and big people
           like presidents,
              kings,
           and professional praying men
              calling Your name,
I feel that my chances of getting your attention
    are about as good as one grain of sand buried under
        a dune on the Pacific Coast
           being chosen "grain of the year"

—except for *one* thing.
    Just one thing!
When you came to visit Earth
You came as a poor man!
You walked among us insignificant ones
    as though we were significant!
    And you heard us
        and brought us relief
        and gave us pride.
        and *You*—
           the God of all those stars
            and of all those leaves
              on
                all those trees

loved us—
    us poor folks!

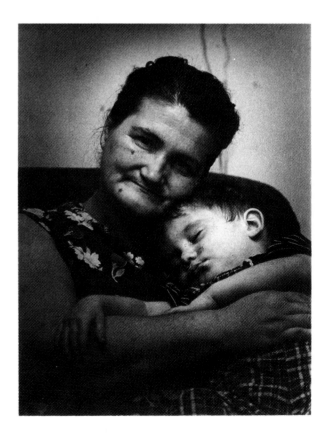

What I'm saying is
    that all I hear from people
        says I don't count much.
But all I know about You says I do.
    You say I've got potential,
        and even if I didn't
            You'd still care.
And I'm hanging *my* hopes on You.

Hear me—
    I'm not asking to be rich
        but I am asking for a little relief
            from the pains,
        for a little more wisdom
            to be me—better,
        and for those who have their heels on my neck
            to understand
                and treat me a little like You do.

I guess my prayer isn't so much for You
    to hear
        the poor
as it is for those in power
                and wealth
    to hear You
and to care about us
    as You tried to tell them to.

She called me. She was
out of food and fuel.
It was Thanksgiving Day.
Her words and predicament
have been much on my mind.

Reverend

How did I get to be eighty
   and
      never
         get over
            being
               poor?
When I was little
   I was poor.
      But playing
      and
         dreaming
      kept some of the pain
        of
          being poor
             away
     and my folks
      kept
         lots of the worries
           from me.
When I was a teenager
   I just knew I'd marry a good man
     with work
      and
         things would be all right.
And I did.
But he was poor, too.

Work was steady for a while,
   but so were the children.

There were good days
   and warm times
      with him.
But there were lots of times
   when his work died off
      and
         his worrying
            brought pain.
He worked any kind of job
   in
      any kind of weather
         till
      the fever got him
         and
      the Lord took him
         and I had to go to welfare.
      Then
         they cut that—some.

Reverend,
   Do people born poor
      have
   to stay that way—always?
Ain't there any other way—
            even when we get to be eighty?
Does "poor" always have to be
      a
         life sentence?

If
I didn't have your face
        to
          press my nose against,
your small body
        to
          melt against mine,
your hand
        to
          grip my finger
               in
                  a search for strength,
your future
        to
          scream that someone needs me—
              really
                 needs me;
If
I didn't have your mother
        to
          wrap me in herself
        at the end of a day
            that
              attacked,
                crushed,
                  exploded,
                    humiliated,
                  hurt,
                    frustrated,
                  and
          reminded me each moment
          of
            the hopelessness
            of
          my ever getting out of the pain of poverty;

If I didn't have you
                to
                  spend my life for,
I wouldn't want life at all.

You see,
    if I didn't have your love,
     I wouldn't have much love at all!
      No purpose.
      No outlet for my hungers.

With you in my life,
    someone needs me,
       loves me,
       counts on me.

In a land where poor men aren't wanted,
    I'm wanted!
I'm wanted by *you*—
    loved by *you*—
         my family.

To a poor man,
    a family is a problem,
        a blessing,
       and a reason to live!

If
    dirt
     and dirty things
        weren't my only toys,
I'd live the kind of life
    you seem
      to understand—
     with the kind of dirt you see on TV commercials,
       the kind that only gets into spots in my clothes
         and then comes out
           with
            the miracle treatment of a detergent.
      The dirt on my body
       would be a "smudge"
     a "cute" dirt that shows, after all,
       that I'm
         all boy.

That dirt is
    temporary,
      adorable,
        instantly removable,
          almost a kid's status symbol.

That dirt is another world. Not mine.

My dirt is imbedded,
         constant,
          smelly,
           disease laden,
          always,
           forever,
            eternal
              dirt.

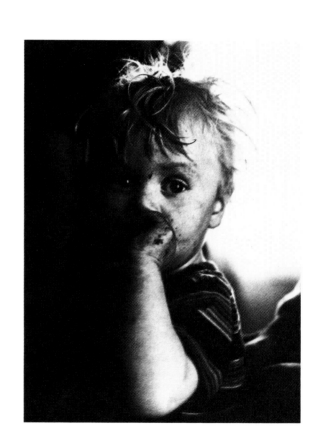

My clothes are washed in the kitchen sink
            -cold water
            -no soap (with my mother, it's always a choice
               between soap or soup)
     the same place where she just washed the diapers
            -cold water
            -no soap
    and where she just washed the dishes
            -cold water
            -no soap
    and prepared the meal,
      -cold water
      -no soap
    and washed the kids
      -cold water
      -no soap.

The same sink—
    food
        diapers
           kids
               clothes
                  dishes.
Dirt may be cute on your kid,
    but it sure as hell isn't cute on us.
And I'm sick.
    Not sick *of* dirt,
        but sick *from* it.
And I don't know how to ever get clean
    —or well.

To a blind girl

To *them*
     like the plastic beer can holder
                    at
                         your feet
     you are a discard.

To *you*
     warm spring winds still brush life into your days,
       school stretches your knowing,
         hugs given and received warm many moments,
          fights with your brother end in justice
                              or
                                in agony,
           tears flow
                    and
                       laughs explode,
          words instruct—and give you a kind of sight,
            thoughts become hopes,
              sounds and touches fill your life.

To *them*
     you are blind.

To *you*
     you are *only* blind.
        All other systems
                       are
                          go!

If
    only Christmas were a time
    when a poor man
      could get away
        with
        the simple
        doing
          of love—
     to say
       in ways that he can handle,
        that he cares.
But the damn bells
   have
      started ringing again
        as enemies
          of the poor.
        Clattering a greed
          we
            can't afford.
        Commercials
         calling my kids to hunger
           for things
             they
               can't have.
Things new only today
   called obsolete by their own makers
      tomorrow.
Toys
   in debt
      to a new gimmick
        —out in April.
           Parts irreplaceable,
           guarantees carefully worded
             and
              unusable.

Homes of the poor
    filled with toys
        unplayable.
    Kept—Just In Case.
It's a great gimmick
    for the manufacturer,
a lot of fun
    for the rich,
a problem
    for the middle class,
but agony,
    pain,
        a continuing, returning grief
    for the poor.
Christmas—
    irreligious people using hymns
        to give their greed
            a
                religious motive.
        Shameless people telling us it's shameful
            not
            to do the "right" thing
            of buying their products
                for our kids.
Loveless people—telling our kids
    that *not* buying
        is equal to
        not loving.
I used to look forward to Christmas.
    Now,
        I'm trapped
            by it.

Inundated,
    my kids can't shake loose from its commercial propaganda,
        and
        it makes me
            inadequate,
            a non-provider,
            an un-lover
                in
                    their
                        eyes.

Even the churches believe
    that
        the only Christian thing to do
           is
              load a kid
                with all the love
                  money
                    can buy.
And if I can't supply the "bought" love,
    they will.
They pass my family's name around
      (a "needy" family)
    and
        after they "check us out" to
          make sure
            we aren't cheating, and
              are "worthy"
              and "deserving"
                of their love,
they collect their castoffs
    from years gone by
      and
    deposit them on us—
outdated clothes that *they* wouldn't be caught dead in
              anymore,
old toys that need "just a little fixing"
(a wheel missing that I could never match,
a transformer broken that I could never fix or replace).
We don't even get to say what *we* want for our kids
              as *they* do.
What we "want"
    is dictated
        by what *they* are willing
          to throw
            away.

They do this
    to teach us about
        the love
           of Christ.
I learned that at Christmas
    Christians
        are angry people:
Angry if your house is too clean—or too dirty,
Angry if they find you have a TV,
Angry if you claim hunger while having three sets of trains
    (given by three different church groups in years past),
Angry if they discover that you sold "their"set
    to buy food,
Angry if they discover that you *didn't* sell one of the other sets
    to buy food,
    and
Angry if you can't show the kind of gratitude
    that
        gives them *their* goodies.
I'm angry too—
    Angry that I can't use my *own* ways
        to show
           my own love.
    Angry that *they* always want to be a hero
        in *my* house
           with *my* kids.
    Why can't they help *me* get the gifts
        and be my own hero
           to
               my own family?
Why do Christians need to fill my Christmas
    with hate
        and my
           hurt?

If
it wasn't for Jesus
I wouldn't be nothin'
      to nobody—except maybe my dog.
Jesus takes some of the pain of "poor"
      off
        my
          back.
It wasn't
    just
      that He was poor—and
        understands *us,*
   or
      that He was rich—and
        understands *them.*
No. It's more than that.
   It's more that He's
      a kind of equalizer,
   and
     without dragging *them* down
   or
    puffing *me* up,
      He reminds me
       that
        we are all as important
         in
         His
          eyes.
And *that* makes a difference to me
   who
    most of the time
     ain't nothin'
      to nobody—except maybe my dog.

Yep,
    I *believe* we are all as important to Him—
        not
            because I need building up,
        but
            because that's the way He is,
        and
            I know that
                that kind of love
                    fits
                        God.
If it wasn't for Jesus,
    this
        always
            being
                poor
                    would be more than
                        I
                      could
                      hold.
But He said
    He
        would never give us more pain
                      than
                        we can hold.
    And He
        was right.
When the weight comes,
    He helps
        with
            the lifting.
Even
    when I think I can see the
        breaking point,
    I see Him clearer
        with
        His strength,
        His love,

and I know He still has hopes for me
                              that
                              move
                              me
                              on.
I think that when He said,
    "Lo, I am with you in *all* the days"
        He even meant days like this one.
    It's a cold day,
        but He gives me another
                        special,
                        inside,
                        steady
                            kind of warm.
Bill collector is coming
                    to scold,
                    threaten,
                    and
                    infect my life.
Jesus is already here
                    to comfort,
                    O.K. me,
                    and
                    infect my life.
With faith,
    even us poor
        can find happy moments.
Because with faith,
    I've got the same "security benefits"
            as Christians
                    who
                        are
                            rich.

God's loving is so good
        that
          it fills in all the rest of
             the
               unequals
        and makes them
         less important
          to me.

When the load starts
   cracking my shell,
I notice that Jesus keeps
     popping
     into my life.
The Cross-Lines kids show up with food
        and help
        and fun.
Pop Knoche, down at the Loyalty Mission,
   for fifty years
     has taught me more about God's love
       than anyone I know.
   Pop's the kind of man
    who feels like God
     to me.
Sometimes I'm even aware of Jesus
   in my church.
  It didn't used to like poor folks like us
     showing up.
  But now its doors are really open every day
   to feed,
    educate,
    love,
  and give itself to
     people like me.

When I saw the job Jesus did
                    on that church,
I knew He was strong enough to
    make a lot of difference—
        even in a life like mine.
In there—
    yesterday—
    I used to just look poor
        and different
            from the rest.
In there—
    today—
    we've all grown
        and are mindful of
            a richness
                we all share
            because we all love
                and
                    are all loved . . .
            and it makes a difference.
Thank you, Jesus.

You cheered, didn't you,
    and "egged on" the welfare cuts.
You knew, you said,
    that it was (what did you call it?)
        a "massive waste of the taxpayer's money."
An elderly woman (heart trouble, diet deficiency)
    was living on $67.50 per month of your
        hard-earned cash.
A 20 percent welfare cut (to teach the cheaters and loafers a lesson)
        brought her $54.00 a month
            (no more medicine or special diet).
            You call $648.00 per year a waste.
Damn it, man!
    You just paid $934 for a rug
        because the old one faded
            in spots.
    Some of you just paid $187,000 for an addition
            to your church.
      (You'll use it once or twice a week.)
Last spring you paid $117 for a suit on sale.
    It was worn four times, but now it's
        A. Out of style
CHOOSE ONE B. Doesn't fit
        C. You really don't like it that much
        D. There are only special times that you can wear it.
I saw in the paper
    where
      a lot of you
        raised $30,000 for a painting
          to lift the spirits
            one notch
              for
            one moment
              of those who might see it.

And
    we aren't really welcome in the places
        where you show it.
    It sure don't do *our* spirits
        that
            much
                good.
From your pile of goodies
    you point
        and holler "WASTE"
            at welfare.
Hell, man,
    think about it.
We ain't the wasters.
    We're just being wasted!
So, when you are
            in that addition to the church
            on that rug,
            wearing that suit,
            looking at that painting,
            or not even using those things,
    Why not do what you've always done for us:
PRAY FOR US.
    It'll show your
            concern.

I wonder if many divorces
                    are
                        like
                            this?
When it finally happened,
    I found myself
        still
            loving
                her
    in a tired,
        hurt,
            empty,
                kind of way.
But being poor
    puts a different kind of pain
                                in
                                your
                                love.
I found that it was
                too
                hard
        to keep
            a
                good,
                    happy,
                        fun,
                            comfortable love going
        when
            I was always
                a failure
                        in
                            her
                                eyes.

We loved
     each
        other   but finally
             couldn't stand the life
               we were giving
                  each other.
And so,
  we both moved on
       to other failures.

The bathing suit
     may
          not
               fit,
but
     the water
          does.

What's tomorrow for?
Does it get to be
                    the same
                                as
                            today?
Do I get to wake up
                on
                    my edge of the bed
                    and
                        in the dim light
                            face the wood strips
                                through the holes
                                in
                                    the plaster walls?
        The same laths
            I faced this morning
                                and
                    every morning
                            that
                                my memory gives me?
Do I get to put on
                that
                dress?
        That *only* dress?
            That too-big
                flimsy
                        worn-out
                            made-for-somebody-in-the-past
                            dress?

Do I get to look my body over
　　for
　　　　new bites?
　　　　　　　Again?
God, how I hate those bugs
　　　and the *new* itches
　　　　　each morning.
If tomorrow didn't come,
　　　at least the itches wouldn't
　　　　　either!
Do I get to wake up to those
　　"happy"
　　　　childhood smells?
　　The kind
　　　that
　　　　　trigger memories
　　　　　　　when
　　　　　　　　you are forty?
　　　The smell of a pile of
　　　　　　stale clothes,
　　　　　-cheap grease baked on an old cook stove
　　　　　　and livened by
　　　　　　　a new flame,
　　　　　-my brother's bandages
　　　　　　-my father's sweat—from yesterday
　　　　　　-the toilet that never flushes right
　　　　　　-the diapers
　　　　　　　-the always wet floor
　　　　　　　　from
　　　　　　　　　always leaky plumbing?
Now that I think of it,
　　would you just
　　　　　　　stuff
　　　　　　　　tomorrow?

If

I were born a flower,
nature
would take care of me.
Rain
and sun
and winter
and spring
would be an acceptable part of life—
not just problems
and pain
to me.
If I were born a flower,
nature would see
that
I was born at the right time—
in the spring
when
the ground nourishes
and
feeds me free
just because I need feeding.
I would live through summer
and blossom
from the evening rains
and give joy—
just
accepted for myself
and
for what I give in beauty.

Weather and food wouldn't be problems.
     Just
          a natural part
             of
          what I need
            in order
               to live
         a full,
            productive,
                no-problem-to-anyone
                   life.

I'd even get to die
    at
        a comfortable time,
            before the unbearable pains
                of
                    the winter of life
                        settled
                            on me.

If I had even been born a dog,
    eating—when I needed it—
    and loving—when I wanted it—
        would be accepted
            as a normal part of my life.
But I didn't get to be born a flower
                or
                    a dog.
I was born people
    and—worse than that—
        poor people.
    And that seems to be
        an unforgiveable offense.
It seems that poor people
    just
        aren't enjoyed
        by those who
            aren't poor.
    We aren't even as accepted
        as a flower
                or
                    a dog.
    Just frowned on
        like a weed
            and
                treated like a cur.
I'd like to be as important
    as a flower
            or
                a dog.

If
    my love for your mother
    hadn't
        given you life
    would you *really* be better off?
No!
    Not to live
        is *not* better than to be poor!
            (Except for a few moments.)
    For out of poor men, too,
        come good men
        and saviors.
    And perhaps I have given the world, in you,
        another savior
            from some problem
              or an ache
                or a hurt
                  or a hate
                    —or two.
If
    you had not been born,
        would
            the world be better—tomorrow?
No,
    because I will give you my love to share
        my patience
        my acceptance of the simple joys
            of
                everyday touches,
                  not expensive,
                  or consumer centered,
                  or money bought,
                  or artificial,

and you can carry *that*
    to those who feel that "better off"
        means
           richer—
           being a larger consumer—in a house and job
                  that causes no one
                    embarrassment.
You see, I found that *they* need
    what we have much of:
        love,
        patience,
        acceptance of simple joys,
        and the ability to face
           and conquer
              the crucial problems of
                a basic existence.
We who are poor
    have much to offer—
        to teach to those who have much—
    about a life not dependent on frills,
    about living through pains far deeper than annoyances,
    about life full of disappointments,
        yet filled by love and the dependence on families.
No, Son, the world is not better off
    without you
        because you are *my* son
           and I offer you to a world
              that needs
                what you will learn
                  and give.

If

you can just stay pretty, Kid,
   you've got your ticket—out!
A pretty face
   can buy you freedom
     even from poverty.
If we dress you up in
     non-poverty clothes,
    teach you to walk "right,"
   to use "right" words
   and mannerisms;
   then take you *away* from your house,
         your family,
         your friends,
   you can be absorbed—
    and *they* will never know.
A pretty face attracts people *first*
  to the pretty face,
    then
      to the person behind it.

It gives you an edge, Kid,
  and
    if you can hide your poverty
     for a moment,
      it buys you *time!*
   Time—
    while they desire you
       as
        a pretty thing.
   Time—
    that they won't give you
     if you are ugly.

Watch carefully how you use that face, Kid.
   It's bait.
      But bait can catch salmon
                  or
                a shark—
    and
     if
       you
         only
           get
              one
                fish. . . .
Girls who don't grow up in poverty
   can
      fall in love
        with
          a guy on their own block.
Not you!
   You have to *calculate!*
   You
      have to use that face
        (a negotiable item)
        not just to catch a good man
           but
              to get you—out.
Your mother—early—
   saw your chance
    and set the tone.
She loves you enough to make you understand that your beauty
        is marketable.
She loves you enough to hate making you marketable.
She
   steers you from the trap
        of
         falling in love
              with
                a neighborhood boy.

How does she teach you to flirt
    without permanently attracting a "local"?
        (To them, you are a rare gem,
               a prize,
                    the girl to catch.)
You mustn't waste your face
             on
             a poor man,
  or
   get
    pregnant
            at the wrong time
                  by the "wrong" man.
It's like this:
When a poor man buys a fancy car,
    he knows that
        the people he wants to impress
           will
             never see his home
               or
                 his neighborhood.
They see him
   and
      his car
      away from his neighborhood.
If they only see him and his car
             shiny
             flashy
   they are impressed—
     or at least
        they judge him by what they see.

Little girl,
   you have a
      Cadillac face.
Don't waste it
   impressing
      a poor man.
It's your ticket—out.
The problem is
   you aren't just pretty;
      you are also nice,
            and honest.
   Can we break you of that
      in time?

Hey

Not-so-pretty kid!
What's your ticket . . .
                    out!
Do you stand a chance?
Do you know what the word
                    "retarded"
                              means?

How are your teeth?
Will any nice young man
                    notice you?
                    Ever hunger for you
                              for keeps?

Can you get pregnant
                    by
                      the right guy
                    at
                      the right time?
                    When he's in a guilty
                              or a marrying
                                        mood?

Will any husband-type
                    ever
                        look close enough at you
                              to
                                  learn to want you
                                    forever?

An ugly
        rich girl
    has
        "rich"
              to offer.
What
have
you
got?

What's your ticket . . .
                    out?

It seems that
the most important word
to
an un-pretty girl
is
"pretty."
A new dress
—even from the secondhand store—
always
pulls out the words that excite her:
"My, doesn't she look pretty?"
Today, while she's small
these words
make her warm
-somebody
-worth something.

But,
how long will the words keep
their "exciting" powers?
How long
before she begins to notice
the
much prettier
always on
somebody
else?

Prostitute?
Well,
if you mean
living with a man
who pays the bills
till he runs tired
—then out—
and
finding another man
to
use me
for
"living" money
to
feed my face
and
the kids,
I guess
"prostitute"
describes me—
and some other housewives.
I hate the name
and the feeling
and
what people think of me.
But when the alternative
is
dying hungry
with honor
—what the hell?
I tried it *your* way (it was *my* way, too).
Married once.
Kids came.
Some happiness.
Then the job went
and
he did, too.

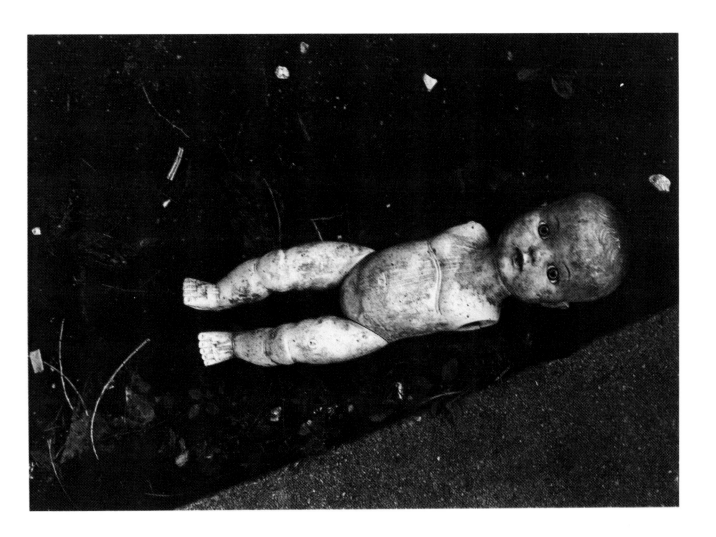

Support came for a while.
    Then less.
    Then no word.
    Couldn't find him—
        so
         I couldn't get divorced.
Friends helped,
    then quit.
Churches gave canned goods, some money,
    then got tired.
I lost the house,
    moved.
Finally, I went to welfare.
    ("Sorry, ineligible. Residency requirements, see?
    Could have got it if you hadn't moved.")
The baby was too young to leave at home
    while I worked.
Never had a skill.
    Third grade didn't teach me much.
Where I lived,
    neighbors were too poor to pay me
            to do their wash.
           No machine
             soap
             hot water
             space
               anyhow.
No bus to take me to work.
    Nobody hiring in *my* neighborhood.
        No way out.
          No one left to help me.
Then came Pete.
    He wasn't much,
        but he loved me
          and
             treated the kids tolerably.

Moved in.
    Paid the rent.
        Bought the food
                and
                clothes.
Wasn't ready to marry.
    Then
    he
    moved
    on.
Somebody else moved in.
I knew that if I was going to feed my young,
    I had to sell
        the
                only negotiable item I had left:
                    me.
All the things you folks told me to do
    to
    keep honest—
    I found out that you
        were
            just talking.
It was *you*
    who slammed
        all the doors.
You talked a lot about honor,
                    respectability,
                    honesty,
                    morality,
                and
                  all
                    that.

Then you shut the doors
                that
                  led that way
                      for me.
I feel bad for what this living
                is
                  showing my kids.
I don't feel like I'm raising them right.
    But
        I am
            raising them!
And I,
    and this body,
        are all they've got to keep them alive
        to *get* raised.
Seems like
    I just ran out
        of
            other choices.
Forgive me,
    Jesus!

The family of poor: Introduction

If
    I only knew
        why
            you hate me,
    maybe
        I could
            make
                amends.
You seem
    to
        want to punish me
            for
                daring
                    to be poor
        and for bringing
            a distant blemish
                to
                    your comfortable
                      world.
Well, Christian,
    let me tell you this:
        If the truth were known,
            I'd really
                rather
                not
                be
                poor!
                      Honest!
Anyway,
    being poor is quite enough of a problem for me.
    I don't think I need your hate
                    piled
                    on
                    it.

The family of poor: Part one

Look, Christian,
    I'm only five years old
        and
            I was
                born
                    to poor folks.
    I don't even remember
        getting
            a choice!
Yet,
    if I had a choice,
        I think
            I'd choose these people all over again.
            Their holding
                warms me.
            Their love puts joy
                in my day.
I don't understand
    "poor"
        yet.
They kind of keep it
        from me.
They don't make me feel poor.
        You do.
And
    I don't know why
        that's important to you,
    or why
        you need to hate me
            for
                being poor.
Will you tell me why?

Will you tell me what you want me to do
         so
                I can get forgiven
              for
                    being poor?
Please tell me *now.*
    I don't think I can always
        stand
            your hate.
Or
    are you going to make me live with it,
    and the questions of it
        all my days?

The family of poor: Part two

Listen, Christian,
    I'm her mother.
        Just think a minute.
            Is it impossible to believe me when I tell you
                that
                I wish to God
                  she
                      wasn't growing up poor?
Doesn't
    that seem
        logical
            to you?
Then why
    is it so hard
        for you
            to believe?

I hear you talk,
   and you act as if
      I
         really *want* it
          this way.
I don't.
Honest!
I hate bringing her up poor,
   lying to her
      that
         these secondhand,
           too-big,
           out-of-style clothes
          look fine
           and
            make her
             pretty.
I hate pumping the same
         cheap
         boring
         fatty
         spiced-to-hide-the-taste
             food
         into her little body
          knowing
         at each meal
          that
           in twenty years
             it
           will take
             its
             horrible
             toll.

Knowing that
                    fat and
                    sick and
                    deterioration
        is what each mouthful
                                    hides
                                        in its
                                            tomorrow.

I didn't think we'd come to this.
My man had a pretty good job
        -two years paid on the car
        -the loan for the house came through . . . .
Then
        the accident shattered his legs,
        healing was too slow,
        they couldn't hold his job any longer,
        compensation ran out,
            then
            the welfare was all he could turn to.
            (How he hated what *that* did to his pride.)
        Then the pneumonia,
        then . . . .
God,
        how I loved that man!
But now
        we've
            got
                to
                    do
                        it
                            without him.
The word for that
                    is
                        tragedy!

And
    I don't understand
        why
           it's important for you
                   to
                     hate
                    me
                      for
                       it!
I really don't need it ....honest!
I really rather he hadn't died ....honest!
I really don't want to raise her poor ....honest!
I really don't like the cold
              hunger
              humiliation
              and hate .... honest!
That all seems so logical to me.
Why is it so hard for *you*
              to
                believe?
Why is it so important
           to
             punish us
                 for
                   our tragedy?

The family of poor: Part three

Listen, Christian,
    I'm eighty.
I hate to tell her
    but
        I've been asking those same questions
                             all
                               my life.

The fact is
   that
      those who hate the poor
         for
            being poor
              don't answer.
Maybe it's because they don't know
        why
           they hate us
       or even
         that
           they hate us.
Today
   I'm in this shack
      made of old doors
         nailed
           together.
      Not enough tar paper to keep the wind out.
        Boards spread on the dirt for a floor.
          Wet wood that I chop—
            then burn
              in this tin barrel
              I use
                for
                  a furnace.
         Smoke in my eyes and lungs—
           and
              no food on the shelf.
And
   I'm still asking:
      Why, America?
         Why is it so important to you
              that
               I
                die
                  in this place?

What is there about you
    that
        savors
            my pain?
All these years
    you've
        been "teaching me
            a lesson"
                about
                    being poor.
I'm eighty now.
Would you care to tell me
    what
        the "lesson"
            is?
No one has ever told me to my face
    what
        I ever did wrong.
No one has ever told me to my face
    what
        I'm guilty of.
No one has ever told me to my face
    how
        to make amends
            for being poor.
Yes, I'm eighty now
    and cold
    and my bones are crinkly.
I probably
    won't be
        around
            much more.
And that's O.K.

I'm tired.
Eighty years of trying to make amends for a sin I didn't commit.
Eighty years of being hated for being poor.
Eighty years of being punished for a series of tragedies.
Eighty years of being taught a lesson.
   O.K.
     It's time now.
     Tell me.
       Just what was it you were trying to teach me
                   for
                     eighty years?

And tell me this:
   does punishment
     for
       being born poor
        have to stay with me
           all
            my days?

The poor use the words
　　"Wait till tomorrow"
　　　　(or next week
　　　　or next month
　　　　or next year)
　　a lot.
Tomorrow
　　(or the hopes that hang on to it)
　　　　are like
　　　　　　a messiah
　　　　　　　　on our calendar.
We think "maybe tomorrow"
　　all
　　　　through
　　　　　　today
　　because
　　　　maybe tomorrow
　　　　　　a door will open . . . out!
　　Or
　　　　"promise"
　　　　　　or
　　　　　　　　"future"
　　　　　　　　　　will finally find a place in my same
　　　　　　　　　　　　　　　　　　　same
　　　　　　　　　　　　　　　　　　　same
　　　　　　　　　　　　　　　　　　　　　job.

　　Or
　　　　the heater will get fixed,
　　or
　　　　a bill will get paid,
　　or . . .
　　　　well, there aren't really many of our hopes that have
　　　　　　　　　　　　　　　　　　　reality
　　　　　　　　　　　　　　　　　　　tied to them.

When I was a kid,
    I looked to the day when
        I would stop dreaming those wild hopes
    and
        I'd be old enough
            to make real life
                out of
                    unreal dreams.
But I still catch myself
        hanging onto dreams—
    and I'm forty.
Sometimes I catch myself thinking
    maybe today
        a big, beautiful car is going to pull up out front
            and
                the rich man is going to get out
                and say,
"I heard about you,
    that
        you are a good man
            and work hard
                and love your kids
                and are down on your luck.
    Here's a check.
    Come by the office. I've got a good job for a man like you.
    By the way, keep the car.
            I see you need one.
            I'll catch a cab back."
Of course,
    he never comes.
I really know
        he
          never
            will.

But, see,
   with poor folks
      even wild hopes
         are
            hopes worth thinking.
               Kind of fun, in fact.
Then, too,
   if we can't have some glimmer
                     in
                        tomorrow,
      even a
         long-shot,
         never-happen
         glimmer,
then each today
                  is
                     always
                        only
                           darkness.

Morning again,
and the fire's burned clean out
again.
Coal will last me through the night
when
it's banked right,
but I never could get
wood
to last.

This time
the cold
seems to be
running
down
the inside
of
my
bones.

I just can't make
this old body
chop
when it's feeling like this.
But—
I've got to
if
I want to make it through
this day.
Sometimes
it's kind of a thrill
just
to wake up again
when
you're eighty-three.
But,
those mornings
when my mind
grips
the cold
and
runs it through my body
I wonder why
God
keeps waking me up
to feel all that
again.

I've had sixty years to touch your hand
   while our bodies moved
      from
         the tense skin of youth
      to
         the sometimes comfortable old sacks
           that
              hold our bones
              and
                 memories.
Sixty years of
   always being poor
      but
   always having the richness
                of
                 each other.
Sixty years of progressing from things like no furnace at all
   to
      the furnace that never works right.
   From the pain our bodies felt
      after
         the agony of
           a working day,
   to the pain they feel now
      as
         they pay the price
           of
              the years that went
              before.

But,
sixty years of melting together
honing
molding
hammering
kneading
and
needing
manipulating
enfolding
loving
each other.
And
it
is
good.

The young search for ways
        to escape
    the pain
        of
            two lives adjusting—
                fearing the loss of themselves
                            in
                            the
                            process.
They too often
    quit
        each other
    before they learn
        the
            trust
                in each other's love
    that allows them to care enough
            to change each other without
        absorbing
            each other.
Maybe
    God
        had a glorious, good thing in mind
            when He said,
                "The two shall become one."
Because if *any* body needs
        another head to help them think,
        another body to warm their nights,
        another soul to help them pray,
    it's us
        poor folks.

I thank God for your patience
in
changing me.
I've lost nothing in the process
of
growth.
Nothing
but some of the tinges
of my selfishness.
Sixty years of you
and
I'm still me,
a changed me,
a me that fits your needs
better.
Sixty years knowing
that
I *belong*
to you—
and *that* doesn't frighten me
at
all.

You see,
   without you,
      I'm not much of me;
and
   without me,
      you, too, are diminished.
Soon,
   one of us must die—
      and the aftermath
         the pain
            the emptiness of the morning moment
                        when I expect your answer
               the waiting for your step
                  the grief—
                     will
                        all
                           have
                              been
                                 worth
                                    it!

For the moments of the
   lonely pain
will always point me
   to the sixty years I had
                  to touch
                     your hand.

The author

"When I was a pastor in New Jersey," says Don Bakely, "I had an understanding with the local 'hoods' (70 percent of whom didn't have fathers) that if they came to church, they could wrestle with me anytime. We had to revise that to anytime except 11:00 a.m. Sunday morning when I was on my way to the pulpit . . . . It was a very physical ministry. One young man said, 'I'd quit this church but where else can I attend church and also beat up the minister?' That man is now himself a pastor."

Now serving through Cross-Lines Cooperative Council in Kansas City, Kansas, Don says, "It's easier counselling with people in the inner city than with those in suburbia. My people don't resort to subtleties and pretense; they tell you the whole story. I have the easy job compared with those who counsel 'sophisticated' people!"

In response to the combined impact of these poems and Terry Evans' photographs, Don mused, "When the day comes down around my people's heads, they can come home and belong to each other."

The photographer

Having taken the photographs in this book, Terry Evans said, "The people who allowed me to photograph them were so open. They didn't try to hide anything. They were honest and straightforward with me. This was such a pleasure . . . . The people I photographed are dealing with survival, not with being able to afford three rather than two cars. They are strong people. Who but a strong person could under such dire conditions continue to love and work and play? There is no room for pity in attitudes toward poor people, but there is a lot of room for respect. These are portraits of some people I like and from whom I have learned a great deal."

Terry is a graduate of the University of Kansas and has shown her work widely. She lives in Salina, Kansas, with her family—a husband, a son, and a daughter.

Photo by Sam Evans